Why Experience

Are you willing to help yourself?

LOU GARY HUGHES JR.

LH Future Investments

W2HY Experience

WHY EXPERIENCE

"Willingness 2 Help Yourself"

Lou Gary Hughes Jr.

Turning Life Questions Into Life Statements

Lou Gary Hughes Jr.

Leaderologist

W$_2$HY Experience
Lou Gary Hughes Jr.

FIRST EDITION

ISBN: 978-1-939288-74-5
Library of Congress Control Number: 2014943075

©2014 Lou Gary Hughes Jr.

No part of this publication may be translated, reproduced or transmitted by any means, in whole or in part, without prior permission in writing from the publisher. Publisher and editor are not liable for any typographical errors, content mistakes, inaccuracies, or omissions related to the information in this book. Product trade names or trademarks mentioned throughout this publication remain property of their respective owners.

Published by LH Future Investments

info@lhfutureinv.com/www.lougaryhughesjr.com

Lou Gary Hughes Jr.

All pictures have links that are identical to the QR Code. Click the picture, use the QR Code or use the link below the picture to see the videos and get an in-depth visual of the W_2HY Experience.

DEDICATION

http://tago.ca/4Ls

Pam, Paige, and Garrett you are my W_2HY.

I dedicate this program to you as part of my legacy. Remember these sayings and may they permeate throughout the next generations:

"Invest in Your Future"

"Invest in Other Peoples Future"

"Effort is Between You and You"

"Choices Affect the Future Generations"

To all who want to change their lives, this program is dedicated to a successful start to this process. It is focused on finding your purpose by getting you to start!

Contents

Testimonials: vi

ACKNOWLEDGMENTS viii

Introduction ix

1 CHAPTER 1

W$_2$HY TIME 7

2 CHAPTER 8

W$_2$HY TIME 19

3 CHAPTER 21

W$_2$HY TIME 27

4 CHAPTER 30

W$_2$HY TIME! 44

5 CHAPTER 45

W$_2$HY Experience 47

W$_2$HY EXPERIENCE WEEK 1 57

W$_2$HY Time 72

W₂HY EXPERIENCE WEEK 2 75

W₂HY Time 81

W₂HY EXPERIENCE WEEK 3 85

W₂HY Time 93

W₂HY EXPERIENCE WEEK 4 97

Appendix 122

Find your W₂HY 122

Finding your Purpose 123

Traits and Characteristics 136

ABOUT THE AUTHOR 138

Testimonials:

"Lou's pursuit of perfection relative to self-development, career development, motivation, role model, spirituality, and as a dedicated family man is very honorable. This book is representative of the aforementioned areas of his character. I wish him great success as he ventures upon this new endeavor."

Lester Piggee
Retired Lt. Colonel, USAF, ARNG

"Paramount family values including profound religious principles. Excellent leadership skills, exceptional mentoring traits, and a very high degree of integrity."

Wyndolyn Jackson
GMAC Branch Manager

"Lou has the capacity to pull out the best in you by showing you how you can accomplish anything by focusing on activities that lead to results. He exploits your passions, changes your belief system to perform beyond your expectations."

Vaughn Johnson
Chief Executive Officer, Painesville Credit Union

W2HY Experience

Lou Gary Hughes Jr.

ACKNOWLEDGMENTS

First, THANK YOU GOD!!

I am humbled at the level of understanding to which you have blessed me. All praises goes to You!
I must acknowledge Pamela Hughes, my beautiful wife. She has always been in my corner guiding me and supporting me physically, mentally, and spiritually. With her the impossible is always possible. She has been the person in my life that has allowed me continued growth mentally and spiritually.
Thank you, Honey!

To my two children, Garrett and Paige, I leave this legacy for you and the next generation. May the Lord bless both of you throughout your lives and use your lives to

"Invest in the Future of Others".

Introduction

Do you ever wish you knew *and* operated in your purpose on a daily basis? Do you wish you could live the entire day with passion and excitement for what the day was going to bring? Do you ever wonder W_2HY few people are successful, and it seems that the majority of the people are not? Who or what defines success anyway? Is it money, fame, family, or job? Success can't be tied only to tangible things otherwise less than 3% of the people could ever define success. It is amazing that some of the people who have the least are sometimes the people who live the most fulfilled lives on the planet. Some people may say it is because they don't know any better or they simply became a product of their environment. Others would say they found happiness in the midst of their trials and tribulations. Sometimes when you are economically or financially challenged you are forced to find other games and extracurricular activities to occupy your time which allows for more creative thinking, games that require exercising the body, and games that require creative cognitive thinking. It is amazing that kids were smarter and healthier before fast food and video games.

What we say typically comes true in our internal belief system!

This book was written for everyone who is always asking W₂HY me; W₂HY does this happen to me? Why can't I prosper? Why is it that I don't feel fulfilled? What am I supposed to be doing with my life? Why do others prosper? This book is also written for the person who wants to refine and verify their W₂HY and leave a legacy. This book is written for the many times you have asked **W₂HY? W₂HY? W₂HY?**

This book is dedicated to *you*, the reader. The goal is to turn life questions into life statements and it all starts with the "W₂HY".

The W₂HY is defined in two ways:

1. The **W**illingness to **H**elp **Y**ourself

2. Compelling LIFE threatening desire and drive to create change

In life we have questions, but **we** hold the key to making a statement. A question has a question mark and gets nowhere without a defining statement, which is always concluded with a period. The period renders a statement as non-fiction instead of fiction. It states *what is* and *what will* be depending on the noun and its adjectives.

What we say typically comes true in our internal belief system.

It is imperative to feed the mind healthy food just as we should nourish our bodies with exercise and nutrition. At some point we should mentally erase the question mark to what we think and want to do and physically insert a period and live the life we plan. This book is dedicated to creating the mental and physical energy to motivate you to **start**! Although there are several well written self-development books in the market, it is my goal to stimulate and inspire you to stay motivated to take action to **START** the self-development process.

The Number 1 reason people fail is because they never start the process. The second reason why people fail is because their "W$_2$HY" is never strongly tied to their passion to stay committed.

It is time to erase the question mark and insert a period in your life. Those who know where they are going typically get there faster!

Why *erase* the question marks in your life and insert periods?

W₂HY?

Everything that feels good is not always good for you. It is time you start fulfilling your purpose! In a discussion I had speaking to 600 people via a conference call I told them, "We can make you feel good on the conference call every Wednesday, but if you don't have motivation with application – **"faith without works is dead."** There is an old TV show, which aired before my time, which featured a character named Otis in the hit series "Andy Griffith Show". He would get drunk, go to the jail, get the key off the door, put *himself* in the cell, lock the door behind him, hang the key on the wall within reach, and would refuse to get out! He had the power not only to free himself, but he held the key to unlocking the **cell of old beliefs** that led to the actions that continued to keep him mentally locked up, bound, and held hostage to start to change. So many of us have several Otis' beliefs in our lives. We know what we should and should not be doing; however, that bad relationship, drug addiction, sex addiction, marriage conflict, business idea, or whatever issue continues to have us bound with uncertain question marks to adhere to change our actions to accept new beliefs. Unfortunately, we seem to operate just like Otis. We do absolutely nothing or change *only* for a moment, get mentally drunk, go back to the jailhouse beliefs that binds us, willingly take the key to the open door to new beliefs, lock ourselves back up in the cell of conformity, and hang the key on the **hook of change** within reach of opportunity to *start* the process of *change*.

You must delete the question mark and insert a period. You have to understand **W₂HY** you do the things you do every day.

You have to make a conscious decision to change!

This requires a strong W₂HY! You have to burn the bridge behind you, arrest the construction workers that built it, and cast away the architect who developed the blue prints. Looking ahead will require new technology and new blueprints for where God is going to take you. It will require **CHANGE, DESIRE, PASSION** and above all your **"W₂HY" (Willingness to Help Yourself)**. In this experience I would like to focus on personal growth through leadership. I have been a student of leadership for over 20 years and understand that **short-lived stimulation we can get from others, but true motivation lies entirely on YOU!**

The W₂HY addresses the leadership skills you need to move yourself forward on your journey to finding your purpose and set the stage that everything **starts with you** and that everything **you do** starts with a compelling "W₂HY", which is an acronym that can be summed up as the *WILLINGNESS to HELP YOURSELF*. It is my hope and desire for you to erase the question mark and insert a period after your W₂HY. You are going to grow and know W₂HY and clearly allow yourself to operate the way God intended so that you can maximize your potential!

...short-lived stimulation we can get from others, but true motivation lies entirely on YOU!

The W₂HY is conceived inside of you. It is in your mind, but most people neglect it, don't feed it and, in some cases, suffer a miscarriage in their future child called purpose. How do we know the "W₂HY" is strong enough to create Definitive Purpose? How strong does it have to be to push us? People say your W₂HY should make you cry. That is true.

However, your W₂HY should be *so* strong it will not allow you to die until you reach your ultimate goal!

Let me give you some examples:

People say they don't have time, but when faced with a LIFE or DEATH situation, they can make time to immediately go to the EMERGENCY ROOM. **The W₂HY** miraculously appears to get stronger – they put a period after the W$_2$HY?

If you have a choice of going in a burning building or call the police, most people will call the police? But, if someone said *your* child was inside, you would not even hesitate to rescue your child. **The W$_2$HY just got stronger - you put a period after the W$_2$HY?**

How about raising $500,000 for a worthy cause. Let's say it is for Cancer Research – most people would not even attempt to raise the funds. What if your child or significant other would die in 2 months if they did not get a series of shots needed to save them that had a total cost of $500,000. The period would definitely be after this W$_2$HY! You would do anything to save your child, mother, father, sister, brother, etc. **The W₂HY just got stronger – you put a period after the W₂HY?**

The same can be seen in everything we pursue in life!

The reason why people start and quit *so* many things is that their W₂HY is WEAK! Their motivation and passion is too *weak* most of the work *week*. This leads to a cycle that causes **stagnation** which leads to **procrastination**. Procrastination causes **frustration** which ultimately joins the majority of the nation with no patience for waiting on the manifestation (i.e. examples: college you started, jobs you quit, relationships you lost, businesses you said you would start or quit). This is W₂HY it is so important to understand W₂HY we do the things we do. This is W₂HY this experience is written to help you understand and grow your W₂HY!

Ultimately, these steps will help you to find your purpose, train your mind by planting seeds of new beliefs, and develop a leadership mentality to lead yourself with the WHOLE goal to pay it forward and lead others to duplicate this experience and help improve the next generation.

1 CHAPTER

LOVE YOUR PASSION
WHAT'S YOUR W₂HY?

This is probably the most important part of the W₂HY. Most people lack passion for anything. It is sad that we get bombarded all day with the bad things that happen, what we see on the news, and read in the paper ... pushed to us through social media, RSS feeds, or via the Internet. Most people are only passionate about watching TV, leisure activities and doing absolutely nothing.

Most people believe they have a time-management problem, when in actuality, they have an Information-mismanagement problem.

Try this tomorrow - Go up and ask people what are you passionate about? Most people would be clueless and shocked as to why you asked! We hope some may say their family or a worthy cause, but most people would not have anything beyond that. They are merely beings walking around on Earth passionless!!

I had an opportunity to visit Rome, Italy. During my visit I realized everybody seemed to be happy about their profession, the food, family, and life in general. They had a since of pride about their work. They enjoyed LIFE! It seemed that everyone understood their role and had respect for the other person and their role in the grand scheme of life. It was an experience I will never forget.

I think many people have lost contact with their inner resources. We live in a world in which everyone around us is telling us what we should do—the government, religious authorities, academic leaders, news media, commercial marketers, our bosses, our parents and now hundreds of friends on Facebook, Twitter, RSS feeds and other forms of social media every day.

I believe the delusion of all these available resources, ideas, and opinions can overwhelm us, put us into a bit of a daze and make us lazy.

Lou Gary Hughes Jr.

As Albert Einstein once said, "Any man who reads too much and uses his own brain too little falls into lazy habits of thinking".

You cannot simply STUDY the wisdom of others. You have to think through ideas yourself and tap your OWN inner wisdom. **The passion** inside you fuels your mind and body to make a change. It is the engine that navigates and runs the **W₂HY**. It makes you do things you would normally think is ridiculous and impossible. It causes clear vision in cloudy times, it provides shelter in stormy weather, it creates calm waters in the midst of the waves, and it creates SO, SO MUCH joy in troubled times... it is the cement of the **W₂HY** foundation... **Willingness to HELP YOURSELF!**

If you have passion it is impossible to make you feel bad about what you are doing.

What causes a man to return to a company he created, which forced him out, only to build the best technology brand in in the world. What passion he had BEFORE he was recognized in public… countless hours he spent researching, creating, people denouncing him, ridiculing him, not believing and now Steve Jobs has created iPhone, iPad, MacBook and who knows what is yet to come from his legacy. He created a culture with his **PASSION** and it will last past his generation. Passion will drive you anywhere you want to go with persistence. Steve Jobs' **W₂HY** had to be strong. He erased the "?", and inserted the ".". He knew his W₂HY and he never looked back no matter the obstacles – he pressed on with persistence.

These questions will identify the things in life you are currently PASSIONATE about! Guess what? They point to what your W$_2$HY is!

W₂HY TIME

¥ What extracurricular activities do you like to do and why? Write at least 3 to 5.

¥ What community service activities do you like to give to or volunteer? Write down 3 to 5.

¥ If time and money was not an issue, what would you spend your time doing all day?

Keep reading to get to the "W₂HY Experience"

2 CHAPTER

LEARN YOUR PURPOSE

FINDING YOUR PURPOSE
W_2HY
(WILLINGNESS TO HELP YOURSELF)

http://tago.ca/Ckm

The W_2HY is a seed impregnated in you! It is in your inner most parts begging for nourishment to grow. If you don't feed it, you will suffer a miscarriage and ultimately terminate your unborn child called purpose. How do we know the "W_2HY" is strong enough to survive and create Definitive Purpose? How strong does it have to be to PUSH US! People say they don't have time, but when faced with life or death situations, funny how they make time to go to the doctor. How do we delete the question mark after the W₂HY and insert the period? How do you, without a shadow of a doubt, know *your* W₂HY?

First you have to know and establish your W₂HY?

You must cast the right net that has the 4 P's – **Passion, Purpose, Persistence, and Principles.** Your Willingness to Help Yourself should always be at the forefront, but if you can't think of any good reasons, please allow me to prime your engine of life and give you some insight.

First Definite Purpose –

Look, if you don't want to help yourself that is a major problem! You **are not** in this world to exist alone – you were put here to make a difference. God gave you a gift, a talent, expertise that is unique for the sole purpose of helping others in this world. If you don't have a strong W$_2$HY for yourself, allow me share some.

How about not letting your kids grow up in poverty – change the next generation if you are financially challenged? In life a "3 Peat" is not always good! We should not be able to look back three generations and see poverty! Somebody has to break that chain! It might as well be you!

How about leaving a toxic relationship so your daughter will know that this is not acceptable behavior from a man!

How about you change your diet so your family, you, the people around you and the NEXT GENERATION after you won't have health issues with diabetes, high blood pressure, or obesity?

How about you start a business so you won't have to continue to live paycheck to paycheck, instead of complaining that the job isn't fair or they don't pay me enough? You are right! It's not fair. It will always be a pyramid! There will always be someone at the top but that does not stop some people from living out their dreams.

As the W$_2$HY gets stronger the HOW gets so much easier because of clarity. Obviously, it requires work, but **once you have a W$_2$HY you have a WILL.** God will bring you resources that your mind couldn't conceive or never dream. The spiritual will over- compensate for the lack of the physical and natural.

You need to accept and embrace the blueprint of your personality, talents, and gifts of your DNA. DNA does not stand for "DOING NORMAL ACTIVITY" or "DATA NOT AVAILABLE" it should stand for Development Needs Analysis. Once you accept your blueprint take the next step to black print. For Christians, it is reading the WORD (BIBLE), reading books, and hanging around people that are moving in the same positive direction that you are moving. **Your primary relationships, or should I say your circle, is a direct reflection of your Integrity, Honesty, and Character.** It is also a direct reflection of your growth both spiritually, physically and financially, as well as, the depth to which you understand how to deal with people and other relationships. **Unfortunately, I have had to learn this the hard way through the price of experience instead of purchased by wisdom.**

I remember years ago when I thought I knew it all. I thought my ideas were always right. I believed, because of worldly success, that if I focused on the next level of success I would always be happy and satisfy all my families' needs. **I had to realize that money could never replace time and that time was more valuable than money.** There was a time when I thought I knew more about church than my wife. I was a student and focused constantly on educating myself in the Word. I pushed my wife to be closer to Christ thinking that I knew more than she did and she actually pushed back by going to another level of spiritual growth! My best friend taught me how to be a better man! She made me think about Definitive Purpose! I am so glad I humbled myself to listen. We would have never made it over 20 years, never had kids that man said was impossible, and I would never have experienced true happiness that money can't buy. My kids make me think about Definitive Purpose every single day. I have created a whole new me over the past 20 years and she has been instrumental in developing my DNA. There is no way we would still be together without a strong W$_2$HY!

Once you have a W$_2$HY you have a WILL!

Know your W$_2$HY by getting to know yourself!!!

Definitive purpose can always be found in a successful person's DNA. You should know what makes you happy? **Get to know you. Court yourself and find what makes you happy.** What gets you up in the morning? Have quality time with yourself. Who better to know you, than **you**? God will provide more for you along the way. If you take one step forward He will take two. ERASE the question mark, insert the period! Make affirmations about where you want to be not where you are – this is called **FAITH**!

Do this simple exercise. It's simple, but powerful. Go to the mirror if you are by one, or wherever you are, say this affirmation/prayer. You are going to confront and empower yourself right now!

You will be talking to yourself, so repeat after me:

I will not quit on you!

I love you!

You were created with a Divine purpose!

God has given YOU ALL the tools to fulfill that purpose!

You have skills that no one else has exactly the way you have them.

The only person that can stop you is you and I will not let you or anyone else stop me from reaching my potential!

YOU will erase the question mark and insert the period.

You will know W_2HY and you will operate above expectations and in excellence. I WON'T LET YOU GET IN MY WAY.....

In Jesus name... Amen...*Your Name* AMEN

Now erase the Question Mark and put a Period after the W₂HY!

You have to delete the question mark after the W₂HY and insert the period – **KNOW YOUR WHY!**

Look around your environment. If you can't change for you, change for your family and for your future generations or the people you inspire. **Remember, there is always someone who sees your situation as a blessing** instead of a bondage situation or circumstance.

Lou Gary Hughes Jr.

These questions will make you think about your purpose in life. There will be an exercise to help you find your purpose later in this experience.

W₂HY TIME

- Do you know your purpose in life? Write down what you think it is and reflect on last week's activities to see if you focused on your purpose.

- Do you feel a sense of accomplishment when you end your day? Write down 3 things you do or you can do to make sure you reflect on each day to benchmark your internal temperature of success.

- Who do you have relationships with, who do you collaborate with daily or who is in your immediate circle of influence? Are they adding and multiplying or subtracting and dividing in your life? You know who is in your circle by the communication and interaction you have with them on a weekly basis. Write down the top five people you communicate with on a weekly basis. This is your primary internal

CIRCLE! This is the sum average of your financial, spiritual, physical and mental future. Take a look around and you will be amazed at the reflection in the mirror of the average of the results.

Keep reading to get to the "W$_2$HY Experience"

3 CHAPTER

LAST WITH PERSISTENCE

LEADING THROUGH DISCIPLINES

If I tell you anything I know, two things will happen with persistence – You will either get to where you want to go, or, GOD will take you higher! I don't know about you, but either option is okay with me.

Don't get tunnel vision – *your* **blessing just may be too small for God.**

The funny thing is most people get what they ask for, deserved or earned!

Persistence requires discipline. Discipline is a rule or system of rules governing conduct or activity.

Some believe for a new house, while others believe for a million dollar home...**HOME** being the key word. Fame and fortune does not guarantee a happy home, but a balance of quality time with the family, balance of work/life and direct mentorship with your kids will affect the future generations.

Some believe for a new car, while others believe for a new Phantom Rolls Royce or Bugatti Veyron Super Sports. Whatever your dream car, yacht, plane, family time, house, etc., you can achieve the impossible by believing **it is possible**. The fight is already won between the 6 inches between your ears.

Some believe for a job, while others believe for a career or a business to replace their job. Who said you have to settle for working for wages when you can work in the daytime for your wages while working part-time on your fortune. Be glad you have job, but be a good steward!!!

The BIBLE is one of the best leadership books of all time.

In the BIBLE it references a good steward is one that invests the 1 talent instead of burying it! INVEST and SAVE!

While you are in the midst of where you are, **who said you would be out of the storm tomorrow?**

Why is it you **think** a lack of persistence should yield microwave results?

It takes time!!! Be patient with yourself - especially if you just figured out your passion and purpose in life. If you have not done so already, right down what makes you happy and focus on those activities. Some people spend a lifetime working on other people's goals at jobs they don't like with people they don't have anything in common. At the end of the day, that is called settling and giving up on your true *potential* for short-term *positions*.

Do you know your "W_2HY"? If you truly had a burning desire that would push you every day you would always have a"." instead of a "?" after the word "W_2HY". Once you burn the bridge behind you on a goal you set, there is no turning back. The reason or "W_2HY" you establish for working toward that goal should not allow you to fail. That is how you know you actually have a strong "W₂HY". As they say, **failure is not an option.** Also, **failure is an inside job** and **people are never your problem – It is you.** Throw away the question mark!!! Insert the period know W₂HY?

Persistence is key! Your persistence tells you if you have lied to yourself and given yourself false expectations. The opposite of perseverance is procrastination. It tells you how serious you are about fulfilling your **passion** and **purpose** in life - don't give up on your dreams and, more importantly, yourself and your family. You affect everybody positively or negatively. You choose every day. Delete the question mark and insert the period. It starts with the man/woman in the mirror leading themselves to do something... setting small goals ... achieving small results that compound over time to achieve BIG results toward fulfilling your purpose in life. I like to call them focus items or focus setting instead of goal setting. Some people get discouraged when they set a goal and fall short.

However, when you incorporate focus setting and you fall short you realize what you have accomplished and you view the journey as progress instead failure.

Don't worry about your neighbors' race!!! You don't know the preparation and probably could not comprehend or handle the sacrifices they went through to survive. More importantly you don't know the plans for their life. Concern yourself with your race!! Erase the question mark and insert the period.

Your passion once harnessed into persistence is like a nuclear time bomb waiting to go off. Once it explodes, as the believers would say, **God will open up a blessing you will not have room enough to receive!!!**

W₂HY TIME

- Write down 3 things that you stopped doing and ask yourself what caused you to stop doing those things.

- Write down 3 new activities you would like to do?

- Take one of the three things you stopped doing and put it to the persistence test to see if you missed any steps.

    - Was it something you desired or were you passionate?
    - Was it focused on helping other people?
    - Did you have small action steps?
    - Did you have a positive attitude in spite of trials and tribulations?

- Did you build a Mastermind Support Group? Who was in your circle of support that could help you achieve your goal?

- Habits come and go. Were you persistently working on it daily regardless of what happened in your life?

Being persistent is the act of showing daily effort.

"Effort is Between you and you".

At the end of the day, you can be stimulated by something or someone, but *ONLY YOU* can sustain daily motivation. That comes from within!

Keep READING!!! You are Investing in Your FUTURE!

4 CHAPTER

PRINCIPLES

LIVING BY PRINCIPLES

Exercising principles in life is definitely easier said than done. There are so many distractions that can take you off course. As a child, your attention span is so short that you can easily get distracted; however, it is amazing that children believe they can do anything until they have been told it is impossible. Nobody is immune to life! The consequences of living make you deal with physical, mental, and sometimes emotional pain; however, a child can get hurt severely and if you don't cry, they will assume that it is normal and quickly stop crying and somehow deal with the pain and move on!!

Imagine if adults had the attitude of a child!

What would he/she accomplish?

How excited would he/she be over new ideas and the possibility of endless opportunities?

"NO" would be a word that *ALWAYS* meant ask or try again until it is "YES!"

Confusion would not exist, because the focus and persistence to ask or try again until they succeed is part of the process.

This chapter is dedicated to running the race during times of adversity by living by principles you set for your life. **Do you realize that you are living at the ceiling or limits *you* have set for your life?** God says that you have not because you ask not. Do you realize if you decide to watch 3 hours of TV every night instead of working on a new business, you have decided that doing nothing is better than doing something to fulfill that dream you have placed on the bookshelf of life? How can you hope to accomplish your dreams by waking up and focusing on the nightmare you call your current routine of life? Wake up and focus on the dream and the dream will eventually become your reality through discovered, planned, compounded actions that lead to results. I would rather die focused on achieved progress rather regretting the attempt due to stagnation and procrastination.

So, what are principles? Let's take a look at the Webster's dictionary definition:

Principle

- A rule of conduct
- A fundamental law underlying truth, basic doctrine
- A belief or set of beliefs of a system, opinion, or teaching

Let's take these three bullets and see what you control. A **rule of conduct** is entirely dependent upon how you choose to act on a daily basis. You decide if you process information positively or negatively. For example, if you are employed and are mistreated at your current job, you decide to respond positively or negatively. Positive could put you in a position to get promoted while negative is bound to make you frustrated and get replaced. How you conduct yourself you control. Principles to live Godly with character, honesty, and integrity will focus your attention on Him not them.

Second, an **underlying truth or basic doctrine**, if established and adhered to, will not allow you to return to your past!

It really is about perspective. Here are some basic doctrines and truths that I have provided as humorous quotes or statements to ponder on:

- I have seen a fool aspire to be King, but I have never seen a King aspire to be the fool
- Water laughs at FIRE unless it is in a pot
- A shark never attacked someone mounted on the wall
- A criminal is always at their best outside of jail
- Infidelity is always an option after divorce

- I have never been afraid of a forest fire outside the forest
- The only time you quit is when you MAKE A DECISION TO QUIT based on your values you set!!!
- Your life is a subtotal of the decisions you make on a daily basis based on principles you set between your ears or should I say fears!
- Your daily GROWTH is the subtotal of the strongest person minus the weakest person in your relationship circle.
- Life can only give you what PRINCIPLES you live by and settle for!
- Think about this: Today you made a decision to read this information right now or later this week. After reading it, you will either do two things based upon your values, principles, and belief

system………. ready……………… **apply or deny** the information!!! Which will you choose

- Twitter and Facebook are filled with people's advice that they fail to use for themselves
  - A plan is always at its best when its friend Action is riding with him as his Road Dawg

Today, you make a choice to *USE*, *ABUSE*, or *LOSE* the knowledge you have acquired. **The next generation is depending on you.**

So how do you harness this focus? To be honest, it is not easy, but the information is found in every nearby library in America. You can do all things through Christ who strengthens you. There is a saying: "Teamwork makes the dream work". The answer is simple:

- Get a **Mentor**

- Get an accountability partner who already has a **Map**
- Surround yourself with a team that is focused and walking in the same direction to help **Manage** the change
- Move beyond standards and have self-accountability by always reviewing progress by looking at the person in the **Mirror**

These four will push you and hold you accountable for the goals you aspire to achieve. It is easy to get sidetracked in the game of life without these four steering you along the way. The best thing is that these four are FREE! These four help you because they LOVE or respect you or simply have LOVE for what they do.

Principles are set in your **internal belief system by external influences you allow based on your values**. The evolution comes, goes from habits, disciplines, standards and ultimately principles. Since habits come and go with lifestyle decisions you make, it is evident that there is a direct correlation to how you respond based on your internal belief system. This diagram depicts it best. Several people develop long-term and short-term good and bad habits, but few people live by principles.

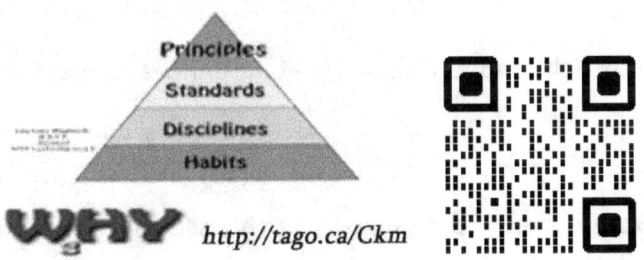

Let me explain and provide 2 brief examples. To do this lets first take a look at the Merriam-Webster dictionary definitions of all 4 stages of growth in the **W₂HY Experience**.

Habits – settled tendency or usual manner of behavior

Discipline – a way of behaving that shows a willingness to obey rules and orders

Standards – ideas about morally correct and acceptable behavior

Principles – a moral rule or belief that helps you know what is right and wrong and that influences your actions

Habits seem to change with the seasons of life. How many habits have you had in the past? How many have you lost? How many were good habits you lost? How many were bad habits you gained? When life changes typically your habits change with them.

Discipline seems to allow circumstances to dictate directional activity. We hear people all the time say I use to work out, now I have kids. Living a healthy lifestyle has nothing to do with circumstances.

Standards have a direct correlation to our environment. Standards are excellent to live by, unfortunately it is relative to our exposure to the environment we are surrounded by. It is about perspective. An athlete in the pros will have an extremely higher standard of a work-out regiment versus someone who plays on the weekend. The standard an NBA (National Basketball Association) dad may have on his son playing basketball will be totally different from a dad who has never played sports. The commitment and workout regimen will be totally different.

Principles have no ties to the environment, circumstances, or seasons of life. A person living by principles has examples of proven steps that they follow to achieve the results they want to obtain. They will only make a change to elevate their work ethic to achieve higher results based on new information. They will never falter, never waiver, and never be swayed by personal circumstances or emotions.

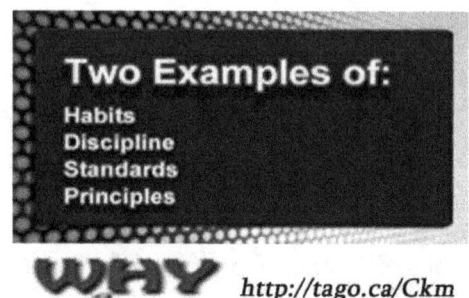

Let's take a look at these two examples:

Habit – I eat donuts every week.

Discipline – I eat donuts only on Fridays.

Standards – I only eat 6 donuts on Fridays.

Principles – I will only eat 2 donuts on Friday once a month based on my commitment to maintaining a healthy lifestyle

Habit – I run twice a week.

Discipline – I run Tuesdays and Thursdays every week.

Standards – I run 2 miles Tuesdays and Thursdays every week.

Principles – I run 2 miles Tuesdays and Thursdays under 12 minutes.

As you can see there is a difference in perspective when you evaluate your commitment level.

W₂HY TIME!

- What are three good habits you use to have? What happened to them?

- What are three bad habits you currently have? How did you get them?

- Name at least one thing that you do religiously every day or every week to self-develop your spiritual side?

- Take one habit that you currently have that you value and turn it into a principle. What do you need to change to take it from habit to principle?

Now it is time to change and modify that belief system to live out your purpose on purpose.

It's time for the "W₂HY Experience"!

5 CHAPTER

"W₂HY" EXPERIENCE

WILLINGNESS TO HELP YOURSELF

http://tago.ca/OJ7

Passion

Purpose

Persistence

Principles

It is time to **Change!**

It is time to take **Control** of your time!

It is time to **Create** a stop doing list and live by a "W$_2$HY To Do List"!

It is time to **Rid YOUR World of Procrastination!**

It is time for the **"W$_2$HY EXPERIENCE"**

It is time to:

- Love your *Passion*
- Learn your *Purpose*
- Last with *Persistence*
- Live by *Principles*

W₂HY Experience

Passion, Purpose, Persistence, Principles

Welcome to the **W₂HY (Willingness to Help Yourself)** *Leadership Development Strategy Experience*, and congratulations on your decision to make an investment of faith and belief in yourself and your future generations. This 4 week experience is designed to move you towards leading yourself instead of being led by life's consequences. The intent is to change your mind set, which will allow the change to take place in your belief system and find your passion to sustain the change for a lifetime.

The Mission is to rid the world of procrastination and get you to start making conscious, compounded, positive *"Choices that Affect the Future Generations"*.

You are not just changing your life, but lives around you and the next generation! You decide whether it is positive or negative every day! Attitude will determine your altitude. The goal is to:

- *Love* what you do by setting small daily goals – **Passion**
- *Learn* your W_2HY – **Purpose**
- *Last* and move beyond habits to discipline – **Persistence**
- *Live* beyond standards – **Principles**

The journey should be fun and exciting to sustain you through the hard times. Life will happen, but the change physically, spiritually, socially and mentally will alter you and your next generation.

So let's get started!

The Questions are below the videos on YouTube. You can look on while you view the videos in YouTube and they are listed starting on page 52.

Questions 1-6 Video

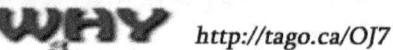

Questions 6-10 Video

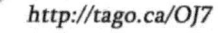

W2HY Experience

Question 11-20 Video

http://tago.ca/OJ7

Before you take this journey ask yourself these questions:

1. Can I take 5 minutes to go to a quiet place to ask myself questions? Make sure you are in an uninterrupted quiet environment.

2. Is my W$_2$HY (Motivation/ Reason for Change) big enough to desire and sustain daily compounded change? *Wanting to change is not good enough! You must have a compelling reason to sustain you through adversity.*

3. Can I humble myself to follow instructions and hold myself accountable and/or get an accountability partner?

4. What are the barriers holding me back from changing?

5. If I changed how would it positively affect my life, my family and the lives of others?

6. What would you do if money and time were not an issue?

7. Am I afraid to fail?

8. Do I have dedicated daily prayer and/or meditation time?

9. Do I need to forgive anyone or myself for past experiences?

10. Have I ever visualized myself succeeding?

11. Do I plan short-term weekly tasks to accomplish long-term monthly or yearly goals?

12. Have I proclaimed my goals to the public or to someone that has my best interest in mind?

13. Do I have an accountability partner who I trust will be honest with me?

14. Do I make affirmations to speak against negative situations in your life?

15. Am I surrounded by people who are at a level based on where I visualized my future destination in life?

16. Am I prepared to be ridiculed for making changes due to my current sphere of influence?

17. Will I be persistent and NOT allow myself to quit?

18. Am I prepared to smile through the difficult times on my way to the rewards God has promised?

19. Am I truly willing to focus on my future and not my past?

20. Now type or write a contract with yourself "That you won't quit on yourself" and send it to someone who will hold you accountable. This will be a person who is able to hear or see your change take place.

This brief journey will take you through **four phases** which make up the **W₂HY EXPERIENCE– WILLINGNESS to HELP YOURSELF**. It is designed to take you where you have not gone before focusing specifically on motivating you to start. The Mission is to rid the world of procrastination. Although there are several programs devoted to self-development and leadership, most of them collect dust due to people's lack of understanding of the process to START:

- **Love your Passion**
- **Learning Purpose**
- **Lasting by Persistence**
- **Living by Principles**

For the next 4 weeks you will discover, plan, act, and set standards to form principles for "living your best life ever" by **starting**! It all starts with you and your willingness to help yourself. Let's stop the problematic procrastination by taking small compounded steps that lead to successful outcomes. This is not just a book or a program, it is an experience!

Let the EXPERIENCE begin.

W₂HY EXPERIENCE WEEK 1

Passion – The First Phase of the W₂HY

Love and staying Passionate Through Adversity

*"Goal Setting 101- NO let's say **FOCUS SETTING 101**"*

http://tago.ca/OJ7

It is week one and you should be extremely excited about the new direction you have on life or a re-focus of energy to love your passion in life.

Passion will be the catalyst for your daily walk and your overall attitude which will determine your altitude.

Any passionate person who has a purpose and a plan **may** get stimulated by others, but they will ALWAYS find the WILL to motivate themselves. It really is that simple. If you are not passionate about something, then the value you place on it will be minimal, which will decrease or alleviate the urgency to complete or start the process.

First, passion has already been created inside of you. The infrastructure is built on planning and FOCUS setting. Make focus setting and planning simple. Focus setting is small consistent steps that lead to BIG results. If you are passionate about something it should show up on your weekly schedule and in your check book or online banking.

Look at how you spend your time and money weekly and there you will find what you are really passionate about.

It is time to make sure you are working on your passion, instead of someone else's passion. This week we work on feeding the passion through planning and goal setting.

To really understand how we think I want to breakdown Focus Setting vs. Goal Setting.

Focus <u>Setting</u>	Goal <u>Setting</u>
FOLLOWING	GET
ONE	ON
COURSE	ANOTHER
UNITL	LEVEL
SUCCESSFUL	

Goals

How many times have you heard people declare New Year's resolutions or set goals that they did not achieve? It definitely takes practice, preparation, planning and a good dose of persistence. Even if you do all of the above you still have to PERFORM. I believe this is the key to achieving goals. Also, what happens to the state of mind of most people who get to the deadline and realize that they are NOT going to achieve their goal? Unfortunately, most people become frustrated and decide to quit.

Most people are not trained on goal setting enough to understand it is a process not a promotion.

To achieve goals you have to:

Practice

Prepare

Plan

Persist

Perform

You don't automatically get promoted to the next level, you have to earn it. Promotions can be obtained at jobs as you progress through your CAREER. Someone decides based on perception that you are either ready or an excellent candidate to represent their organization at the next level. Goals involve a process you achieve through a **set COURSE** of actions. People often need training to understand how to set goals and have realistic expectations of achieving the desired results. Because of this, most people never set goals. Unfortunately, a vast majority of the people who do, without the proper expectations and planning, get frustrated and most of them give up or venture off in a new direction. I am glad I read an article by James Clear on Entrepreneur.com who suggest that Goals are actually at odds with Long-Term progress. One thing that I found interesting is that in every successful Billionaire and Successful Coach, they posted the goal, but they focused on the systems! They focused on the activities that would eventually lead to the results. They FOCUSED! So what is focus setting?

Focus-Setting

Focus setting is **Following One Course Until Successful**. Focus is defined as directed attention towards a point of concentration. What absorbs most of our energy on a daily basis is what harbors our attention. We must direct that attention to focus on what will give us the results we seek. It is a fact that focusing on 20% of the desired activity will yield us 80% of the results we seek on a daily basis. Focus setting can easily be broken down into this simple formula. There have been several articles written in Forbes online, Washington Post, Harvard, and the University of Utah proving that we can't Multitask. David Strayer, a cognitive psychologist at the University of Utah, tells Psychology Today - "Our brains don't do two things at once; instead, we rapidly switch between tasks, putting heavy burdens on attention, memory and focus". All studies point to people who have intentional focus perform at higher rates getting results quicker than those who attempt to multitask several task at the same time. They say the human mind really does not multitask it switches. This causes a loss of 40% in productivity of the prior task. For example, if someone is working on a project, checking emails, and answering the phone they could

get distracted by the phone calls. If a perceived emergency phone call takes 30 minutes away from the project and email takes another 30 minutes, it could take up to 30 more minutes to regain the focus needed to get back on track to complete the project. So here is a simple formula for focus setting:

1. Only focus on 3 things a day
2. Spend 30 to 45 minutes each working on the 3 things for the day
3. Make sure you take at least 10 minutes to break away completely from what you are working on. Don't check email or take phone calls – do 100 push-ups, take a walk, meditate in silence, or simply sit back and take a 10 minute nap
4. Start the process all over again with another 30 to 45 minute segment. For resources go to http://lougaryhughesjr.com/page/why-leadership-resources
5. For WHY To Do list check out the resource page.

The more you focus the faster you will achieve results and the closer you will reach your end result.

Don't begin before you plan.

Always begin with the end in mind. Long-term goals are achieved by completing small planned tasks compounded over time - Daily, Weekly, Monthly, and Yearly. Let's start with the basics. This is why I embrace "Focus Setting".

Don't start tomorrow until you plan it today.

Plan tomorrow by writing down the activities you want to accomplish from the time you wake until you sleep. For now, focus on the top 3 things that if they were accomplished would give you the most gratification or a sense of accomplishment for the day. I believe this is a good place to simplify and explain focus setting.

Focus setting

Imagine you set out on a family vacation. What would happen if you did not have a map and you did not know where you are going? You are bound to get lost, frustrated and you may NEVER find your destination.

Setting goals is the map and focus setting is the compass to what you value and what matters most in your life.

If you don't have a planner, get one or use any free App on your phone, but use something – a piece of paper will work for today if you don't have anything. Here are some examples of what you can use:

- Microsoft Outlook

- Any online App on your Smartphone or tablet

- Google Plus

- Day Planner or Franklin Covey Planner

- Franklin Covey has an online planner

- Microsoft Word has Calendars and Planners

When you know the outcome you can focus on results.

http://tago.ca/OJ7

NOW, WE START DREAMING AGAIN!

If you had only 30 seconds to write down 3 things/accomplishments/ goals/ aspirations that you want to accomplish – what would they be? Take 30 seconds to write down 3 goals.

Same exercise, but now you have one day to live. You have the power to have anything your heart desired. Nothing is off limits.

If you had only 30 seconds to write down 3 things/accomplishments/ goals/ aspirations – what would they be? Take 30 seconds to write down 3 goals.

Keep this, you will refer to this again.

What do you want people to say about you at your funeral? These probably will be the things you value the most.

The statistics say that most people will probably have things listed in the following three categories:

- Family
- Spiritual
- Finances

Time to live your life with a purpose **on** purpose. Time is **not** on your side. No one knows the hour or the day, but one thing is a fact - **100% of the people will die**. What you do with the time you have is critical.

Time to get acquainted with your W_2HY?

Motivation starts with you and the desire and understanding of your life's purpose. To truly understand and know your life's purpose, you have to get revelation and understanding on your God given gifts and how to use them to help others. Time to get to know yourself.

Get a journal or something to write on. Spend the next few days having fun dreaming again. Write down everything you want to do, where you want to go, or what you would like to accomplish.

W₂HY Time

Finding or strengthening your Passion in LIFE

- Write down things you like to do.
- Write down the God-given talents you possess — we all have them.
- Prioritize 3 talents you value or appreciate the most.
- Your purpose will always be defined by the ability to add value to other people's lives based on your gifts and talents you already possess.
- Write your mission statement. Resources for personal mission statement below from easiest/simple to more in-depth. Take time now to go to

Appendix page (52) to find your W$_2$HY. Other resources below:

- **Find your W$_2$HY!** Go to Resource Center and download <u>Finding Your Purpose document</u>
- Another resource for mission statements
    - <u>Earl Nightingale Mission Statement Builder</u>
    http://www.nightingale.com/mission_select.aspx
    - <u>Mission Statements Resource Online</u>
    http://www.missionstatements.com/index.html
    - <u>Franklin Covey Mission Statement Builder</u>
    http://www.franklincovey.com/msb/

Post in areas where you can see both the VALUES and the MISSION STATEMENT so you will see it and read it daily. Pray about your purpose.

PLAN FOR NEXT WEEK

Take 15 minutes to schedule time on your calendar for 1 hour next week or 2 thirty minute time slots to plan time to complete WEEK 2.

W₂HY EXPERIENCE WEEK 2

PURPOSE – Second Phase of the W₂HY

"Learn Your Purpose - W₂HY"

http://tago.ca/OJ7

The only way to truly operate in excellence is to operate with a Divine purpose. To maximize your potential you will need to tap in to God-given talents you possess to fulfill your destiny. The only way to be in total sync is to know your W₂HY! There was story told some time ago of a construction worker who always purchased building materials. He was a master at buying the best equipment and supplies and his plans for the buildings were ingenious. The supplies he purchased were imported from the most expensive cultures overseas, handcrafted from most of the ancient cultures. HISTORY artifacts you could say from the best craftsmen in the world. However, he never built anything and died without one single building. He failed to START.

IS YOUR W$_2$HY STRONG ENOUGH?

What is the definition of the W$_2$HY?

W$_2$HY = WILLINGNESS 2 HELP YOURSELF

It is a compelling reason that forces movement, desire and passion, thus, forcing inertia and ultimately continuous momentum. Some real life examples may be:

- Early Retirement
- One or both parents staying home to raise the kids
- You or your spouse wanting to leave a legacy for your kids after death
- College Fund
- Foundations or charities to help homeless, foreign aid, cancer, etc.
- Career or Business
- Health
- Terminal illness
- Financial Freedom
- Time Freedom

The W$_2$HY should be strong enough to feel like a life or death situation. It has been said that your W$_2$HY should make your cry or it simply is not strong enough.

Your W$_2$HY should have:

- **Passion** – will weather you through the storms
- **Purpose** – motive that will keep you focused
- **Persistence** – will saturate your thoughts and delete "can't" and "if" from your vocabulary
- **Principles** – will demand all actions and thoughts to operate based on honesty, character and integrity despite life conditions, emotions, physical or mental states behind closed doors

A **W$_2$HY** always keeps a toolbox full of old and new tools of progress and success. Now let's assess your toolbox.

Do you have a system that tracks your appointments and task daily?

Do you set goals or as I like to say focus items?

Do you know your purpose in life?

Do you feel a sense of gratitude when you come home?

Do you have a team of advocates?

DO NOT GO ANY FURTHER WITHOUT HAVING A SYSTEM TO TRACK APPOINTMENTS AND TASKS.

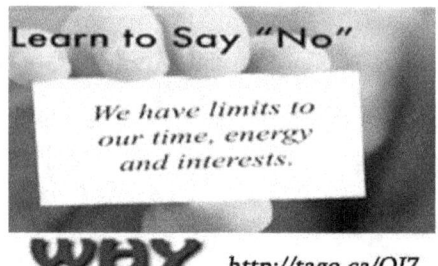

W₂HY Time

Let's set some goals, scratch that, let's do some Focus Setting!!!

Prioritize your goals based on what you value the most **(refer to week one)**.

- First, delete any goals that conflict with your VALUES and MISSION STATEMENT – these are called distractions. So, make a "STOP DOING LIST". That's right, stop doing some things that are distracting you. Moving forward, you will ONLY make a "**W₂HY To Do List**". This list is small and ONLY includes things that must be done after based on your understanding of W₂HY this will impact your goals and aligns with your values and beliefs. Anything else on the list of "To Dos" is a distraction.

- Prioritize your goals based on order of importance - 1 year, 3 year, 5 year, etc.

- For the W$_2$HY Experience our focus is on starting the process, so focus on 1 year goals.

- Take 30 minutes to solidify your 1 year goals. Make it fun and reasonable. Use this simple method for goal setting (**STORM** method). Here is an example:

    a. **S**pecific – I will read leadership books(list the books)

    b. **T**argeted – Eight in one year

    c. **O**bservable – Decide how you will get the books (Kindle, Hard Copy, PDF, etc.)

    d. **R**easonable – Two every 3 months (per quarter)

    e. **M**easureable – Track my results weekly by reading 30 minutes Monday and Wednesday

- Calendar the major events in this order

a. Vacation and family time first

b. Business/ Work related events

c. Other events

¥ Practice compounding small daily steps while preparing to perform big:

a. Take your top 3 goals

b. Block out a 30 minute time slot this week to work on your top goals this year

c. Here is a basic example of buying a new house

i. I want to buy a home, in Avalon subdivision in 2 years on MM/ DD/ YYYY at TIME

ii. I will own 2 investment properties in downtown (city, state) with 2 year lease tenants with options for them to buy on MM/DD/YYYY at TIME

d. Here is an example for fitness

   i. I will be at 198lbs by MM/DD/YYYY at TIME by running 3 times a week and participating in 2 cardio and one yoga class per week

   ii. I will run a 7 minute mile on MM/DD/YYYY at TIME

¥ Next week we learn to change by going beyond habits – we change through discipline and staying the course.

W₂HY EXPERIENCE WEEK 3

Persistence – the third phase of W₂HY

"Leading through Disciplines"

Welcome back and get ready for an awesome week!!!

There comes a time in your life when change is inevitable. However, discipline can implement boundaries that will not allow you to detour from major goals, values, personal/family goals you set for your life.

Habits can be broken, but discipline is a choice.

Discipline is not glued to feelings. It states the obvious, but changes the outcome. "It is the two bars that keep your wheel straight in the carwash of LIFE". The choices you make are purely tied to choices that have been created by the disciplines you practice daily in your life's journey. This week we make decisions. **No longer will we embrace "fence post" mentality**. You are either on the side of the fence making a choice to change or you are on the other side refusing to change.

Definition of Discipline: behavior in accord with rules of conduct; behavior and order maintained by training and control. Discipline is a conscious choice you make to do something even when you don't feel like doing it.

Habits vs. Disciplines

Habits

Almost everyone hears that doing something 21 days forms a habit. This may be true, but this is NOT good enough. To prove it:

- How many times have you stopped doing something you used to do all the time?
- How many times have you told yourself – I used to be good at that?

Habits can change any way the wind blows. Habits change with life events and circumstances. When life happens, habits tend to change direction without your consent.

Disciplines

Disciplines are choices. They are conscious decisions to work to create expertise in a particular area. Disciplines are managed and controlled. They are refined, groomed, practiced, and managed to achieve consistency in the practice of that particular focus area. Conscious decisions CAN change behavior.

Let's take a look at the history of disciplines to truly understand the concept. I like the Wikipedia Free Encyclopedia definition because it walks through the history. Here is an excerpt:

Educational institutions originally conceived of "disciplines" to catalog and archive the new expanding body of information produced by the scientific revolution during the early modern period. Curricula and disciplinary designations were linked first in German universities during the first half of the nineteenth century. By the approaching 20th century, these were gradually adopted in other countries and became the accepted conventional subjects. In the sciences, these included physics, chemistry, biology, geology, and astronomy. Social science disciplines include economics, politics, sociology, and psychology.

Prior to the 20th century, categories were broad and general. The term scientist was coined in 1834 and was not popularly used until the late 19th or early 20th century. With rare exceptions, practitioners of science tended to be amateurs and were referred to as Natural Historians and Natural Philosophers, designations that dated back to Aristotle. Natural history encompassed what was to become the life sciences; natural philosophy became the physical sciences.

Few opportunities existed for science as an occupation outside of the educational system. As specializations developed, they did so hand in hand with the subjects identified as modern scientific disciplines in universities. Science as a profession was coupled with educational occupations. Higher education provided the institutional structure for scientific investigation as well as economic support. As the volume of scientific information increased with unprecedented speed, it became fruitful to concentrate on smaller fields of scientific activity and specializations emerged. Academia's identified disciplines set forth the organizing structure and forums for like-minded people of specialized interests and expertise. The most significant manifestations of this were the scientific journals.

Over time, disciplines evolve and connect. For example, botany has now become a branch off of biology, and paleontology has ceased to exist in the academia world. It has become primarily a museum science. As old disciplines dissolve into broader categories, new disciplines have emerged from the primary disciplines, such as biochemistry.

With this concept in mind we see why discipline is mandatory to maintain the level of success you desire. If the advanced academia refer to these as disciplines because of advanced continued studies, this should provide evidence of the required sacrifice needed for success in any particular area of your life. Now let's practice discipline.

Lou Gary Hughes Jr.

W₂HY Time

Let's Practice Discipline!

Discipline requires accountability and consistency.

The #1 reason people don't change and lack discipline is due to their poor use of time management and their lack of understanding of emotional intelligence.

Most of the mismanagement stems from the mismanagement of information.

Practice discipline this week and gain 31 hours back of your time by:

- ¥ Turn off the TV for 1 hour a day – get back 7 hours
- ¥ Get up 30 minutes earlier – get back 3 ½ hours

- Cut your lunch short 15 minutes – get back 1 hour and 45 minutes

- Focus on one thing at a time – don't allow distractions to interrupt you from what you are working on unless it is an emergency – get 3 ½ hours. Multitasking is a myth

- Shift work time(time you arrive and the time you leave) when others are not in the office if possible – get back 5 hours

- Don't answer the phone. Have a set time for returning or accepting phone calls – get back 3 ½ hours

- Have a set time to check email – get back 3 ½ hours

- Have a set defined time for social networking – Facebook, Twitter, etc. – get back 3 ½ hours or more for some people!

Let's Practice Discipline! <cont.>

Next week discipline yourself by planning activities in the following areas. Make sure you practice but act like you are performing discipline. Make it happen! Here are some examples:

- Physical – Example – Work out 3 times a week
- Mental – Example – Read a self-development book for 30 minutes a day(could be 15 minutes in the morning and 15 minutes in the afternoon)
- Social - Example – Network with family members and non- family members
    1. Make a phone call
    2. Take one person to lunch
    3. Send a card
    4. Send an email

5. The choice is yours

6. Spiritual – Example – Read the bible 10 minutes for 5 days - develop spirituality

Next week we learn to live beyond STANDARDS!!

We learn to live by **PRINCIPLES!!!**

Leadership Book Recommendation – Purchase the download or buy the book "The Compound Effect" by Darren Hardy.

W₂HY EXPERIENCE WEEK 4

Principles – Final phase of W₂HY

"Living by Principles"

Welcome back!

You have reached week 4 and I am extremely proud of you. You should feel a sense of pride and gratification. Understanding your purpose, harnessing your passion and practicing discipline will open up doors that will allow you to be a true servant leader. In order to start and keep the momentum you must operate under the authority of principles that will not allow you to go back to your old mentality.

Definition of Principle:

Rule of conduct. A standard or rule of personal conduct. A fixed or predetermined policy or mode of action.

Definition of Standards:

Those morals, ethics, habits, etc., established by authority, custom, or an individual as acceptable.

Habits can be formed, but may change with the changing of life.

Standards are a choice to change and consciously exert effort to maintain change.

Principles require standards that provide you a level of living through disciplines, to which, you refuse to settle for less than the standard(s) you set. Your mentality will not allow you to live below that level.

Your mentality receives a doctrine and now it is at a level of principles.

Living by principles requires being:

1. **Definitive** in defining the culture – Surpassing the Standard
2. **Devoted** to faithful thinking (Faithonary) – Have FAITH that it will happen
3. **Determined** by having a contingency plan – Failure is not an option. What is the plan when things don't go the way I planned?
4. **Dependable** by being accountable
   a. Track your success weekly
   b. Get an accountability partner
5. **Diligent** to compounded small daily task moving from daily activities to short-term goals to long-term goals to the ultimate VISION

6. **Difficulties** arise when you work with imperfect people. Especially as it relates to TEAM efforts
    a. You can't do it alone
    b. You have to share ideas
    c. Forward momentum can't halt for short-term praise
    d. Accountability to yourself and others
    e. Resources via people assets
    f. Not everyone will be happy for your success some people will be jealous.
7. **Dedicated** in re-defining the culture to maintain relevance

In order for true success to take place I will break each one of these requirements down to provide clarity.

Definitive about the culture.

To truly understand the foundation of living by principles you have to understand the culture of the principles you desire to live by. This will be a defining moment in your life. This is not just a perceived standard of living it is a level of ambitious visionary thinking that very well may be beyond your current level of thinking and living. However, these principles help to explain the cultural level and expectation you should aspire to obtain.

Culture

- Inherited ideas, beliefs, values, and knowledge, which constitute the shared bases of social expectations of living

- Activities and ideas of a group of people with shared traditions, which are transmitted and reinforced by members of the groups continued development and growth
- The artistic and social pursuits, expression, and tastes valued by a society or class, as in the arts, manners, dress, conduct,
- Behavior, expectations, etc.
- The minimum level of growth with the expectation of continued improvement that is mandatory behavior of the entire group.

For example, it is expected that all lawyers pass the BAR. It is expected that all agents in Real Estate have a license. These are standards that are requirements and expectations to perform in their field of expertise. The standard is to graduate and get a license, the principle is to operate with integrity, honesty, and character while upholding the laws and regulations that govern the position. In all cases the people who adhere to higher levels beyond the standard who operate with honesty, integrity, and character outlast quick fame of those who meet the standard but fail to honor their position with lifelong principles established by those who have paved the way before their generation. The way has been paved. The people who paved the way, expect you to move beyond standards and set new levels that will dictate future principles for others to live by with higher levels of achievement.

This week we change your mentality and psychology about life. This will require continuous ongoing learning. It will require change. It will require a change in the way you perceive the outcome at the end of the destination. It will require you to define the culture. Although change does not happen overnight, it is always worth it!

Devoted to Faithful Thinking – Faithonary.

Once you definitively define the culture you can now embark on faithful thinking. Notice I did not say visionary? I have no problem with visionary thinking, but for the sake of having a definitive WHY, you must move past vision to FAITH. Let's contrast the definitions of visionary and faith to truly understand the difference

Definition of Visionary Thinking

Visionary

1. Given to or characterized by fanciful, not presently workable, or unpractical ideas, views, or schemes: a visionary enthusiast.

2. Given to or concerned with seeing visions.

3. Belonging to or seen in a vision.

4. Unreal; imaginary: visionary evils.

5. Purely idealistic or speculative; impractical; unrealizable: a visionary scheme.

Definition of Faithful Thinking

Faith

1. allegiance to duty or a person or one's self: loyalty

2. fidelity to one's promises (2) : sincerity of intentions

3. belief and trust in and loyalty to God (2) : belief in the traditional doctrines of a religion

4. firm belief in something for which there is no proof (2) : complete trust

5. something that is believed especially with strong conviction

Faith has to be prevalent. Visionary thinking focuses on what *could* be, while faith is focused on what you believe the outcome *will* be. Being definitive allows the bridge to be burned with a purchase of a one way ticket to your destination.

Determined by having a contingency plan.

Everyone that is successful had a contingency plan called "Don't Give Up". It was their only plan "B". It is silly to think that what you are really passionate about you would even consider failure.

You want to hear determination? How about a young man growing up in Ohio, who moved to Michigan. Some of his siblings died due to sickness. The sickness eventually caused him to be death. He was home schooled. As his hearing deteriorated he viewed this as a gift because he had less distractions. Just imagine how much we are distracted today due to all the accessible technology at our fingertips? He said he could enter into deep sleep uninterrupted without outside noise. As a teenager he opened two stands selling newspapers and hired other boys to run them. Since his primary job was working on a train, he used his profits to secure a laboratory. After rescuing a child from a rolling freight car his reward for saving the child's life the child's father taught him the skills of being a railroad telegraph operator. He was only 16 at the time. This eventually led to his first invention which was an electric vote recorder in 1869. Now from improving the telephone, inventing the phonograph and several other inventions he racked up 1093 patents. To this day no one has topped his record. I would have to say Thomas Alva Edison was determined. He is most recognized for his endless attempts at revolutionizing the light bulb. We know he tried over 1000 times to create what most people take for granted each and every day. It is safe to say he was determined!

In order to reach the gold at the end of the rainbow you must understand that luck does not exist in success, you have to have a heavy dose of determination and focus to the end result in order to reach gold.

Dependable by being accountable for your actions.

What you do when the doors close and in private really tells you about your character and integrity. Being dependable is all about trust. The question is how much do you trust yourself? Will you commit to yourself? In order to hold yourself accountable you have to track your progress to make sure you are adhering to your commitments. Tracking your progress allows you to evaluate whether you are on track or if you need to modify or make changes immediately to stay focused on the end result. Sometimes it is an excellent idea to have an accountability partner who is moving in the same direction or who has your best interest in mind who will hold you accountable to your commitments. I am not surprised that Olympic athletes break records during the Olympics. There seems to be another gear that can only be accessed when there is competition or accountability from someone who has your best interest in mind. If you are going to live by principles being dependable towards others as well as to one's self is critical.

Diligent toward daily compounded activities that lead to results.

Daily activity really points towards where your passion lies. If you think about it, let a week go by, evaluate your progress, and you will realize that you either had determination or deterioration. You were either determined to stay diligent towards your goal or you suffered more deterioration towards ever seeing or achieving the result. I am reminded of the awesome book by Daren Hardy titled the Compound Effect. In this book he talks about taking compounded daily activities or steps towards reaching your goal. He points to the daily activities that will either lead to your desired result or the opposite desired result. It is not the french-fries that contributes to obesity, it is eating them 2 days a week over the course of 2 years that takes a toll on your body. Conversely, it is the consistent savings of only 1 penny compounded over 30 days that yields over $5 million dollars. Most people would take $10,000 today vs. a promise of $5 million dollars in 20 years. This is the way compounded interest works every day. This is also the way our lives work every day. If we use the same formula and spend a small amount of time every day working on our focus items, imagine how much closer we would be to obtaining the prize! It is impossible to work on something every day diligently and NOT become an expert.

Difficulties arise when you deal with imperfect people.

You can't expect perfect moments from imperfect people. Just because people let you down, you can't sacrifice your principles to appease someone else's agenda. Difficult times will always come up when you have to work with other people. It is not just because they despise your efforts or they become jealous of your success. Sometimes it is just because they have their own agenda or they may not know how to deal with the situation. Maybe they have never been taught how to live with character, honesty and integrity. Make sure you are careful not to judge without remembering where your journey brought you from. It will take a good team to help you with your dream. You never know who God will align you with short-term for long-term results.

You won't and you can't do it alone. There will be people who will stimulate old ideas, introduce you with new and improved streamlined processes and align you with new people that will help to complete your journey. Sharing ideas is essential to long-term success. I have seen it time and time again people who get tunnel vision because they feel they have reached success and that their way is the only right way to do something. The problem with this is that people change and times change. What worked last year may not work this year. What was popular ten years ago, may be unacceptable in the present. Basically, you can't rest on your laurels and fixate on short-term praise. It will stop your forward momentum and in some cases cause you to stop growing all together. For example, years ago I use to belong to a Baptist church. It was growing at a rate of 10% per week. We moved 2 times during a 7 year span from one location to another. There were so many ministries growing we had to expand a third time in year 9.

However, they stopped holding themselves accountable and lived under the assumption that revenue growth and membership growth overrode principles and they fostered an environment of liabilities instead of people assets.

People began to look away and refused to hold people accountable including the deacons and the pastor.

Unfortunately, success got the best of the church because they realize they had arrived. The problem with arriving is that you think you made it, and once you believe you arrived, you don't need the map, directions, you never embrace new ideas since you have, in your mind, completed the journey.

The church looked over unethical practices, never considered the ideas of young adults, and they believed what worked in the beginning got us here, so the church stuck with them. As I fast forward 30 years, the church has split 3 times, several preachers have been fired or removed. The original church has basically come full circle and has less members than it had when it started the growth process. In the beginning they were open to sharing ideas and focused on the people. Without adapting to the change in the younger generation and respecting their opinion, eventually the growth of the church halted. No new people, no new ideas, no more attraction, no more growth.

If we can remember that people can be assets or liabilities than we would be willing to treat people with respect and value their opinion. You never know who may be willing to help you for free or who God has placed in your path to help you reach your goals.

Dedicated in re-defining the culture to maintain relevance

If I could use the analogy of going to the doctor, I would say *dedication is the medication*. Most of the time, if you are sick, the doctor will write out a prescription for the symptoms of your particular ailment. The symptoms point to the illness and a prescription is written to counteract the symptoms. The ailment has to run its course. Sometimes it seems that you get worse before you get better. Sometimes your body has to create enough anti-bodies to fight the sickness. You are getting relief from the symptoms. Antibiotics are given to fight infections and either inhibit or kill bacteria. Most people simply catch the *unfaithfulness bug*. They become sick with *disloyalty flu* towards their focus or mission. They lose their focus and they fail to adhere to the principles that will develop and prepare them for their continued growth. I am writing you a prescription of *"Dedication codeine"* which should be taken at least twice a day with a full glass of *patience*. I would not take it on empty principles with no organization rest.

The best way to stay dedicated is to do something every day and make sure you check in to make sure what you are doing is relevant to today's culture while maintaining the integrity of your mission. Doing the right thing all the time is not easy. It is easy to read a book and apply absolutely nothing and say, "That was an awesome book!". However, it is wishful thinking at best that air automatically causes you to breath. Air just supplies the oxygen. You still have to breathe it in. What a travesty to gain knowledge and fail to apply it. How sad it would be for someone to give you a million dollars only to be able to view but never spend the money. This is your opportunity for application and supplication.

So let the games begin. Have fun and it starts with the 4 P's:

- **Love your Passion**
- **Learning Purpose**
- **Lasting by Persistence**
- **Living by Principles**

Today you make a conscious decision to change behavior. To start the process of change. Although the road will be a mixture of hills, valleys, curves and various side roads highways and by-ways, you have decided to live by PRINCIPLES. There is no turning back.

Success is:

success

n.

The achievement of something desired, planned, or attempted

It is time to RID your world of procrastination and make

"Choices that Affect Your Future Generation"

Suggested audio:

Download and listen to "The Strangest Secret in the World" by Earl Nightingale. Listen to CD one only <u>The Strangest Secret Earl Nightingale</u>.

Download the Law of the Seasons by Jim Rohn [Season of Life by Jim Rohn Success Store](#).

Listen to these two in order to understand how to maintain principles you set and the benefit of personal growth as it relates to your future and the "Future of the Next Generation".

W₂HY TIME

Living by Principles

- If you have not done so already, complete the activity Finding Your Purpose page 132.
- Daily activity to live by principles
    a. For the next 2 weeks complete the WHY to do list the night before
    b. Review before you go to bed to prepare for the next day

Appendix

Find your W₂HY

Finding your Purpose

Defining your Purpose / Revelation about your Purpose

These questions are designed to get you to think about your purpose in life. Many people struggle with this question on a daily basis. I believe everyone has a purpose in life to educate, motivate, stimulate and provide guidance in this life to benefit others to reach their God-given potential. It is in our ability to help others where true gratification, happiness and a sense of accomplishment can be found. This revelation is what some people come to know and is defined as SUCCESS! Understanding your purpose in life will allow you to help yourself, but more importantly to help others. Let the journey begin.

Defining or re-defining your sense of gratification and self-worth

A. I feel the most gratification and sense of self-worth or I feel like I make a difference in this world when I....

Basically, what gets you excited? List 5 to 7 things you like to do. For example:

1. **Leadership Training**

2. **Public Speaking**

3. **Writing**

4. **Teaching and Mentoring Others**

5. **Exercising**

6. **Reading leadership information to educate and present to others**

7. **Thinking of new ideas to develop leaders**

B. If I were not limited by time and resources and I knew I could not fail what would I choose to do every day? List 3 to 7 activities. For example:

1. Help people with their career and/or business plan
2. Entrepreneur workshops on various topics related to business and self-development
3. Help people find their purpose in life
4. Provide a blue-print to change their mindset in reference to "Attitude, Awareness and Action"
5. Rid the World of Procrastination by teaching the START process
6. Church leadership training on self-development and policies and procedures
7. Help non-profits reach their full potential by providing a network to help them with their cause

C. Narrow the focus to 3 from the 2 list above. Do this by answering these questions:
   1. Which of the above do not involve helping other people? Mark these off the list.
   2. From the remaining, choose the top three I could do every day even if I never received any compensation or recognition. These will be the foundation of your passion and purpose.
   3. Top 3 Focus Areas
       i. **Invest in the Future of others and non-profits through leadership training via my network**
       ii. **Help people find their purpose by understanding their WHY**

iii. Help people START the process of change. Mission- "Rid the World of Procrastination

Getting to know your current value system and how it supports your focus and purpose.

D. What are the top 7 characteristic traits you feel you portray that you value the most?

1. Entrepreneurship
2. Honesty
3. Integrity
4. Character
5. Health
6. Family
7. Spirituality

Here are some examples of traits listed below on page 5: Traits and Characteristics

Based on these what are your top 5 that really define your legacy? Circle the top 5.

Now, based on what you value the most do any of your values conflict with your top 5 "Focus Items"? Your values should not conflict with your Focus Items. If they do, you may need to re-evaluate and modify what you value the most.

For example, if I am focused on becoming a personal trainer, I should value exercising and eating healthy.

If your focus items are supported by what you value the most, you have most likely figured out your purpose in life.

Now what 5 focus items can you perform every day that will move you closer and allow you to track your progress to ensure you achieve results? For example, based on the above focus areas and what I value the most, what will I focus on doing on a daily basis to support my purpose:

1. **Reading**

2. **Writing**

3. **Public Speaking**

4. **Exercising**

5. **Thinking**

These focus items should be in your daily planner and you should have time allocated to ensure you do these things on a consistent basis. Please see the example of the "WHY Leadership To Do List". You can create your own or allocate time on your calendar, but make sure you write it down and allocate this time on your calendar. You can tell a lot about what people value by reviewing their check book or bank statement and where they spend their time on a weekly basis. No matter what they say, where you spend your time and how you spend your money is the true indication of what matters most in your life. This is why it is so important to understand what you value the most to ensure you allocate time and resources to have experience achievement and success. Now that you have an example, it is now time to create/ define/ redefine your purpose.

Living on Purpose

A. **I feel the most gratification and sense of self-worth or I feel like I make a difference in this world when I....** Basically, what gets you excited? List 5 to 7 things you like to do:

    a. _____
       _____

    b. _____
       _____

    c. _____
       _____

d. _____

_____

e. _____

_____

f. _____

_____

g. _____

_____

B. **If I was not limited by time and resources and I knew I could not fail, what would I choose to do every day?** List 3 to 7:

a. _____

_____

b. _____

_____

c. _____

_____

d. _____

_____

e. _____

_____

f. _____

_____

g. _____

_____

C. Narrow the focus to 5 from the 2 list above. Do this by answering these questions:

    a. Which of the above do not involve helping other people? Mark these off the list

b. From the remaining, choose the top three I could do every day even if I never received any compensation or recognition.

c. **Top 3 Focus Areas**

   i. _____
       _____

   ii. _____
       _____

   iii. _____
        _____

D. **Getting to know your current value system and how it supports your focus and purpose. What are the top 7 characteristic traits you feel you portray that you value the most?**

   a. _____
      _____

Lou Gary Hughes Jr.

b. _____

_____

c. _____

_____

d. _____

_____

e. _____

_____

f. _____

_____

g. _____

_____

Now what 5 focus items can you perform every day that will move you closer and allow you to track your progress to ensure you achieve results? For example, based on the above focus items, every day I focus on doing the following:

1. _____

2. _____

3. _____

4. _____

5. _____

Traits and Characteristics

Adaptability	Appreciation	Attentiveness
Availability	Commitment	Compassion
Concern	Confidence	Consideration
Consistency	Contentment	Cooperation
Courage	Creativity	Decisiveness
Deference	Dependability	Determination
Diligence	Discernment	Discretion
Efficiency	Equitableness	Fairness
Faithfulness	Fearlessness	Flexibility
Forgiveness	Friendliness	Generosity
Gentleness	Gratitude	Honesty
Humility	Integrity	Joyfulness
Kindness	Love	Loyalty
Meekness	Mercifulness	Observance
Optimism	Patience	Peacefulness

Perseverance	Persistence	Persuasiveness
Prudence	Punctuality	Purpose
Resourcefulness	Respect	Responsibility
Security	Self-Control	Sincerity
Submissiveness	Tactfulness	Temperance
Thoroughness	Thriftiness	Tolerance
Trustworthiness	Truthfulness	Virtue

WHY Experience

2014©

ABOUT THE AUTHOR

Born June 1, 1967 in Little Rock, Arkansas, Mr. Hughes was raised with a focus originally on athletics. Work experiences led to 20 plus years in Corporate America traveling around the United States and abroad. His focus has always been on giving back to the community and providing direction to others to achieve their goals. An eight year Veteran of the Armed Forces coupled with influences from his grandmother from an early age, have both forged disciplinary skills that motivated him to create disciplines of Honesty, Integrity, and Character.
Throughout the years Mr. Hughes continues to seek out opportunities to:

- **Serve on Non-Profit Organizational Boards**

- **Assist with new entrepreneurs who aspire to improve the world**

- **Create multiple streams of passive income**

- **Create legacy businesses that will provide future opportunities for the next generation**

- **Live with Honesty, Integrity and Character**

His mission is to:

"RID THE WORLD OF PROCRASTINATION"

Today, Mr. Hughes is focused on Leadership Development Training, Partnering with Non-Profits, and Passive Income. He hosts several Entrepreneur Workshops annually and he is dedicated to getting people to START the process of "Investing N Your Future". He has created an experience called the **"W2HY EXPERIENCE"** that allows you to:

- Learn your **Purpose**
- Love with **Passion**
- Last with **Persistent**
- Live by **Principles**

Lou Gary Hughes Jr.

He is the creator of the W_2HY. "Willingness to Help Yourself" currently known as the W_2HY EXPERIENCE! The W_2HY mission is to "Rid the world of procrastination".

He is known by some as the Leaderologist and Leadership GURU and continues to help both adults and young adults through self-development and living with integrity, honesty, and character.

Some of his favorite quotes:

"Effort is Between You and You"

"Choices Affect the Future Generation"

"Invest N Your Future"

"Failure is ALWAYS an INSIDE JOB"

"START" Study Training And Required Test

His Core Values:

- **Humility**
- **Fitness**
- **Entrepreneurship**
- **Financial Security**
- **Creativity**
- **Contribution**
- **Character**

Community Involvement

- W$_2$HY Leadership Cares
- LH Future Investments
- RehabTime C.O.O.
- Board of Directors - N.H.C.F
- Board Member - Logistic Council
- Board Member - Workforce Investment
- Board Member/ VP - National Sales Network

- Board Member - Beautification Committee

- Alpha Phi Alpha, Fraternity Inc. - Life Time Member

- Founder - Individuals Concentrating on Education - AR

W2HY Experience

W2HY Experience
Lou Gary Hughes Jr.

FIRST EDITION

ISBN: 978-1-939288-74-5
Library of Congress Control Number: 2014943075

©2014 Lou Gary Hughes Jr.

No part of this publication may be translated, reproduced or transmitted by any means, in whole or in part, without prior permission in writing from the publisher. Publisher and editor are not liable for any typographical errors, content mistakes, inaccuracies, or omissions related to the information in this book. Product trade names or trademarks mentioned throughout this publication remain property of their respective owners.

Published by LH Future Investments
info@lhfutureinv.com/www.lougaryhughesjr.com

Lou Gary Hughes Jr.

www.ingramcontent.com/pod-product-compliance
Lightning Source LLC
Chambersburg PA
CBHW052035070526
44584CB00016B/2047